A book of daily devotion and reflection one day at a time

JANET STEPHENS

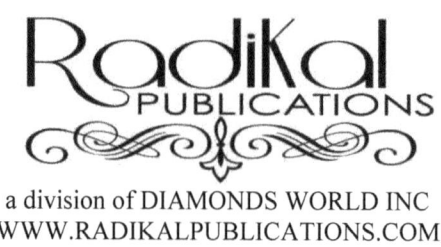

a division of DIAMONDS WORLD INC
WWW.RADIKALPUBLICATIONS.COM

Copyright © 2017
JEWELS BY LADY J
JANET STEPHENS
Editing: CLARKE COLUMBUS CONSULTING
Printed in the United States: First Printing
All Rights Reserved

This book or parts thereof may not be reproduced in any form, stored in a retrieval system or transmitted in any form by any means-electronic, mechanical, photocopy, recording or otherwise-without prior written permission of the publisher, except as provided by United States of America copyright law.

All works within are the creative property of the author; and no part of this book may be performed, reproduced, stored in a retrieval system, or transmitted by any means, electronic, mechanical, photocopying, recording, or otherwise, without the expressed, written permission of the author.

Dedication

This book is first and foremost dedicated to God. Without Him I would not be alive to write about these powerful nuggets. It was Him who graced me to walk through each one individually as these are all points of victory for me.

To my husband who loved me before I actually had victory in these jewels that I'm sharing. I am eternally grateful for every push you have given me to be my best self for God, for our family and for the Kingdom. You are a trusted voice.

To my children, all 6 of them but especially my daughters, these are the Giants I slayed for you so you wouldn't have to.

To the women that I pour into whether you are directly connected to my Jewels Women Ministry or not, this is for you. Many things I do or say is to help you to see what God sees when he looks at you. He is especially fond of you.

To my parents who are no longer here, I know you would be proud of me. It's an honor to be your daughter. Mom you said I was going to be a star, a star for Jesus or a star for the devil. I chose Jesus.

To my siblings, the blood ones, the God-ones, the made up ones (I crack myself up), and my friends (I only have 2 best friends) y'all know the real me, the spoiled me, the real testimony, the real victories. Thank you for always supporting me.

To my spiritual mom, Apostle Lynette Appling who saw me as a Jewel before I did, who loved me when she had every reason to not cover me and who continues to challenge me to mature. NO MORE VICTIM.

Last but not least to Clarke Columbus Consulting for editing and my new sista Shirelle "Diamond" Hogans and Radikal Publishing. She is the real MVP. As a professional you put up with all my shenanigans including overdue assignments. As a friend, you listen, you let me be ugly for 60 seconds then remind me of my assignment. You are irreplaceable. I'm so glad we crossed paths.

Annnnnnddddddd so I don't get in trouble for naming names, as there are so many, I just want to say thank you all those who continue to pray for me, to those who prayed for me and preyed on me. It's all working for my good. I'm at the table. (smile).

Table Of Contents

Dedication ……………………………………… 3
Introduction …………………………………….. 8

Citrine
    Day One: Not A Product Of My Past…………….. 11
Ruby
    Day Two: Love On Another Level ……………… 15
Sphene
    Day Three: You Are More Than A Conqueror 19
Labradorite
    Day Four: Freedom Is A Choice …………………. 23
Mystic Quartz
    Day Five: Grass Greener On The Other Side? …… 26
Aquamarine
    Day Six: Transformation Requires My Whole Being 29
Agate
    Day Seven: Freedom Is A Choice ………………… 33
Seraphinite
    Day Eight: The True Integrity Of The Heart ..…… 37
Mother Of Pearl
    Day Nine: Well Done …………………………….. 41
Peanut Wood
    Day Ten: Live And Learn ………………………… 45
Orthoclase
    Day Eleven: Giantslayers ………………………… 49

Diamond
    Day Twelve: Guaranteed Victory …………………… 53

Sphalerite
    Day Thirteen: Go Get The Wealth …………………… 57

Flourite
    Day Fourteen: Fear Go! ……………………............... 62

Carnelian
    Day Fifteen: Jehovah-God …………………………... 66

Jade
    Day Sixteen: God Can Be Trusted …………………… 70

Sapphire
    Day Seventeen: I Am Not A Victim ………………… 74

Silver
    Day Eighteen: Don't Fall For The Trap! …………….. 78

Sunstone
    Day Nineteen: His Reflection ……………………….. 82

Afghanite
    Day Twenty: Be Healed And Move On! …………….. 86

Turquoise
    Day Twenty One: When God Does It ………………. 90

Zircon
    Day Twenty Two: What's Your Value? …………….. 94

Shellstones
    Day Twenty Three: If ……………………………….. 98

Malachite
    Day Twenty Four: Healing Is Ours …………………….. 102
Garnet
    Day Twenty Five: You Just Do You …………. 107
Calligraphy
    Day Twenty Six: You Are A Designer's Original .. 111
Cavansite
    Day Twenty Seven: The Finish Line ……………. 115
Apatite
    Day Twenty Eight: It Doesn't Feel Good,
                       But It's For My Good ……. 119
Ammolite
    Day Twenty Nine: It's No Secret, I'm Pregnant! . 123
Natural Amber
    Day Thirty: Don't Get Tired! …………………… 127

Meet The Author ……………………………...…… 131

Introduction

Malachi 3:17 And they shall be mine, says the LORD of hosts, in that day when I make up my jewels…….

Definition:
Jewel-
    1. a precious stone, typically a single crystal or a piece of a hard lustrous or translucent mineral, cut into shape with flat facets or smoothed and polished for use as an ornament
    2. A person or thing that is treasured

While putting together this small, yet substantial, short, yet powerful book of devotion, I thought about how precious we are to God and how closed we often are to receiving the unconditional love He extends to us. We are, indeed, His jewels - precious in His sight - and He sees us better than we will ever see ourselves. I pray that while reading this book of devotion, you will receive a glimpse of His constant, unfailing love and will begin to see yourself in the image of God.

We often experience things in life that begin to cut deep into places in our hearts that should have been treasured and safe. As a result, our hearts can become hard. What really should happen is we should allow what the enemy meant for evil, the words and actions of others that were meant to harm, discourage or diminish us, to cut us into shape smoothing and polishing us so we come out of the situation as "pure gold." You shouldn't look like what you've been through - you should look like a Jewel prepared for the Glory of God - an ornament.

Prepare to transform your mind and your life through these short yet powerful Words of encouragement and empowerment. I often tell others if what is said steps on your toes, say ouch and keep moving. But, as you keep moving, do something different and use that "ouch" moment as a teaching moment to help you learn, grow and develop. If you do this, the enemy will never again be able to trip you up with those same old tactics, for you will have grown beyond them and will be able to walk in victory!

At the end of each devotion, there is a note section for self-reflection where you can write your own thoughts to help process what you have read.

These are moments with God speaking to me that I have made transparent to share with the world. Now, **let's grow!**

Jewels
by Lady J

CITRINE

Named after the French word for lemon, citrine is yellow, gold or orange-brown transparent quartz.

Day One
NOT A PRODUCT OF MY PAST

Repeat after me: "I'm not a product of my past, and I leave the grave and every dead thing behind me". -LaKeesha Leonard

Often, after we have repented, we still allow our emotions to keep us in the memory of the sin, the event which in turn causes you to feel shame, guilt, fear etc, even though God has forgiven us. In essence, we beat ourselves up. Satan can only do what we allow him to, and he can only affect what we give him access to.

With that said, remember, it's not always the devil - more often it's YOU. Have you ever heard the saying, 'crying over spilled milk'? Well, THE MILK IS SPILLED, NO GOOD, YOU CAN'T SCOOP IT UP and IT'S OF NO USE! The same goes for your past - as long as you have given it to the Lord. The past only becomes your present when YOU reach back for it either literally, emotionally or mentally. Remember, it was Lot's wife who looked back and became a pillar of salt, but it is God who says, to the one that is truly repentant, that he will throw our sins into the "sea of forgetfulness" and remember the sin no more.

In Proverbs 26:11 that reads, "As a dog returns to his vomit, so returns a fool to his folly or, in another translation, so a fool returns to his stupidity." In this context the vomit is your old, dead, stinky and vile past. Leave it where it belongs, don't reach for it and don't look back. So today, choose life, and speak life!!!

Afterthought

1. What people/places/things continue to remind you of your past?

2. What scriptures will you pray that will remind you to walk in Freedom?

3. Finally, choose to be free in Jesus' Name!

Ephesians 6:10
Finally, my brethren, be strong in the Lord,
& in the power of His might

Reflection

RUBY

Ruby is the red variety of corundum, the 2nd hardest substance on the Mohs scale, with a rating of 9. It is the combination of hardness and rich color that makes fine ruby so valuable.

-Day Two-
LOVE ON ANOTHER LEVEL

We definitely have this love thing twisted. Oftentimes, we love people based on how we feel. Sometimes, we love them based on how we receive love. Other times we love people based on how they have loved us or how others have loved us. Sometimes, we even love based on what we think they need. *HAZARD SIRENS* BEEP BEEP BEEP!!!

According to John 15:12, Jesus commands us to love one another as HE has loved us. Mannnnnnnnnnnnnnnnnnnnnnnnn think about that! Take a Selah moment... do you remember all the times you have disobeyed God, backslid, totally walked away from Him, lied, cheated, stole, and YET GOD'S UNFAILING LOVE WAS EVER PRESENT? This thought hit me like a ton of bricks!

I encourage us all to go back to the drawing board and ask the Lord to help us to love as He has loved us. When we love like that, all hatred, malice, vengeance and ill-will has to depart from us as we are extending the same love to others that God extends to us - even when we don't deserve it.

Afterthought

1. What are your thoughts about love?

2. What prevents you from loving on this level? (As Christ has loved us)

3. What are some things you are still holding onto?

4. Do you believe that you can let those things go?

1 Corinthians 13:4-8

⁴ Love is patient, love is kind. It does not envy, it does not boast, it is not proud. ⁵ It does not dishonor others, it is not self-seeking, it is not easily angered, it keeps no record of wrongs. ⁶ Love does not delight in evil but rejoices with the truth. ⁷ It always protects, always trusts, always hopes, always perseveres. ⁸ Love never fails

Romans 8:37 (KJV)
………<i>in all these things we are more than conquerors</i></p>

Reflection

SPHENE

Sphene, also known as titanite, is a gem with a dispersion higher than diamond. Specimens of high clarity can be cut into gems with a brilliant fire. Its softness limits its use to earrings, pins, pendants, and low-abrasion jewelry pieces.

− Day Three −

YOU ARE MORE THAN A CONQUEROR

You see, to conquer something means to:
1. Gain or subdue by force
2. To gain or secure control of

You see, not only do you have the ability to conquer but you have the ability to be more than a conqueror, to do more than subdue, to do more than secure control of ... you can do MORE than that! By your decision, perhaps just one decision, you can totally change your life. You can totally change a generation! Yes, perhaps you remained a virgin, perhaps you didn't have a baby out of wedlock, perhaps you never got high or drunk, but that one decision has now made you more than a conqueror. You changed the course of a generation. You broke generational curses, generational addictions and generational poverty. Your children are free, your children's children will never experience lack, your children's children will walk in the favor of the Lord, you are MORE THAN A CONQUEROR! You are more than just average, you are a cut above the rest - a priceless, a jewel "with a dispersion higher than diamond".

Afterthought

1. What things have you identified as mountains in your life that you need to conquer?

2. What are the barriers that prevent you from experiencing full freedom?

3. How will you know that you have conquered a specific issue in your life? What will that look like?

*In all these things we are triumphantly victorious
due to the one who loved us*

Galatians 5:1
Stand fast therefore in the liberty wherewith Christ hath made us free, and be not entangled again with the yoke of bondage.

Reflection

LABRADORITE

A gemstone from the plagioclase feldspar family that produces flashes of iridescent blue, green, yellow, orange, or red when moved under incident light. This luster is known as labradorescence.

Day Four
FREEDOM IS A CHOICE

I declare that the women of Jewels will choose to be free. You see, God will not go against your will. You can choose to stay in bondage, to stay broken, to stay connected to the wrong people, places and things, but you can also choose to be free. Today I believe that you are a unique jewel that can no longer be kept in a box. The box is broken today and you are walking in your liberty!!!

Afterthought

1. What does it mean to be free?

2. How much will your freedom cost you?

Galatians 5:1
Stand fast therefore in the liberty wherewith Christ hath made us free, and be not entangled again with the yoke of bondage.

John 15:16
Ye have not chosen me, but I have chosen you, and ordained you, that ye should go and bring forth fruit, and that your fruit should remain: that whatsoever ye shall ask of the Father in my name, he may give it you.
.

Reflection

MYSTIC QUARTZ

Mystic Quartz is the product of a new high tech enhancement process, whereby a coating is applied to colorless quartz.

GRASS GREENER ON THE OTHER SIDE?

Don't assume the grass is greener on the other side. Remember, snakes are amphibians that have the unique ability to change the color of their skin based on their surroundings. **What you may think to be greener grass could, in fact, be a field of snakes.**

OPEN THE EYES OF YOUR HEART!

Afterthought

1. In what situations are you most tempted to believe that the grass is greener on the other side?

2. What personal characteristics do you need to observe to discern the real integrity and character of a person?

John 10:10 (NKJV)
The thief does not come except to steal, and to kill, and to destroy. I have come that they may have life, and that they may have it more abundantly.

Reflection

AQUAMARINE

Aquamarine belongs to the gemstone family of Beryls. Origin of name Latin "aqua" meaning water and "mar" sea. Aquamarine is usually free of inclusions and possesses a superior brilliance. The more intense the color of an Aquamarine, the higher its value.

TRANSFORMATION REQUIRES MY WHOLE BEING

I am transforming daily by the renewing of my mind! I am complete, I am whole and I lack nothing.

My mind, my will, my emotions, my desires and my passions are in alignment with God's will, with God's Word and His plan for me.

As my mind transforms, my speech and eventually my actions align with my purpose.

My purpose is to please God and live a life that brings glory to Him.

God created all of me and through a life that is submitted to God I am transformed in His Image, and I become His delight.

Afterthought

1. What are you devoted to do on a daily basis to keep your mind on the Lord?

2. How do you know that you are God's delight? Document some things that God has said to you. Write them down to create a memorial so when the enemy tries to tell you lies, you have something to remind you that you are God's delight.

3. Imagine being God's delight, what does that mean to you?

Psalms 23:1
The Lord is my shepherd I shall not want

Luke 10:27
And he answered, "YOU SHALL LOVE THE LORD YOUR GOD WITH ALL YOUR HEART, AND WITH ALL YOUR SOUL, AND WITH ALL YOUR STRENGTH, AND WITH ALL YOUR MIND;

Reflection

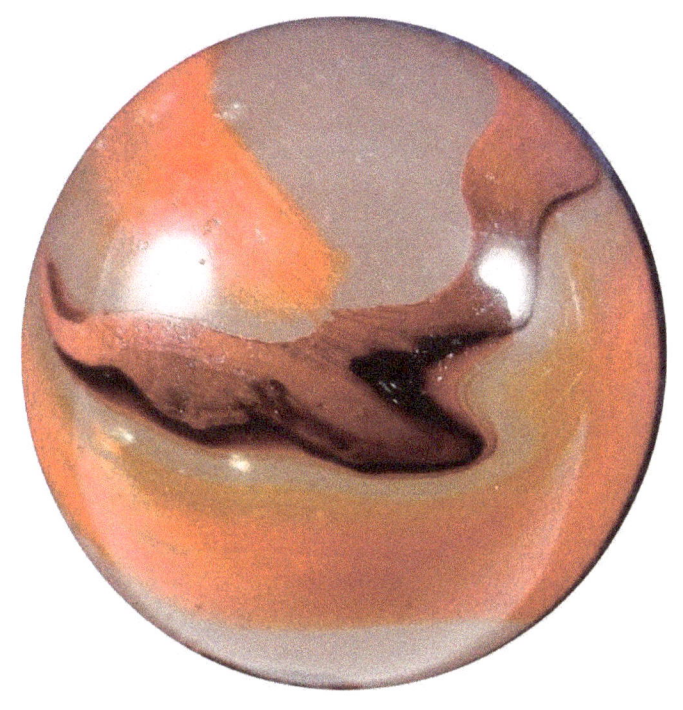

AGATE

Agate is a gemstone found in many continents from Brazil to Afghanistan to Australia. It is popular for necklaces as the stone has many natural patterns and comes in a variety of natural colours. It can also be dyed to obtain interesting colours. Tribal civilizations have used agate as necklaces for thousands of years. Agate gemstone is one of the oldest gemstone on record, from biblical days as agate jewelry and as decorative agate bowls.

-Day Seven-
FREEDOM IS A CHOICE

The scripture says to be "transformed by the renewing of your mind." This scripture is not talking about your brain - it's talking about your soul. Your soul (the seat of your mind, will, emotions, passions, desires) must be transformed. Why the soul? I'm glad you asked, because once you get saved your spirit is sealed, but your body is obedient to however you direct it. We direct it according to our own will, our own desires, our own passions and our own emotions. Imagine a body following a soul that is submitted to God. That's why we must constantly declare the will of God and then make our soul submit to the will of God. We can't just declare and then live the same. Our actions must match our declarations. We can no longer continue to mindlessly recite declarations and decrees.

God's Word says we will be held accountable to every Word and thought. When you release a Word over yourself, there is an expectation that your life will align with that Word. That's why we say my mind, my will, my emotions, my desires and my passions are in alignment with God. God's will and his Word do not contradict. But, anytime our will resists the direction of God and His Word, we must know that it is our job to pull that thought, that desire and that mindset down to obey God. When we do that, we will walk in God's plan for us. His plan is, "Beloved I wish above all things that you may prosper and be in health even as your soul prospers."

That means our whole being is walking in prosperity and we lack nothing! Like on Jeopardy - "I'll take transformation for 2500."

Afterthought

1. Take some time to think about declarations you have made. Does your life line up with that Word? Why or Why not? Are there any declarations or decrees that you need to recant?

2. Honestly inspect your mindset. Are there erroneous thoughts that you have been basing your life on that do not align with God's Word?

3. Are there areas in your life where you can identify that God's Word and your life are in contradiction? What are you willing to do about it?

2 Corinthians 10:5
Casting down imaginations, and every high thing that exalteth itself against the knowledge of God, and bringing into captivity every thought to the obedience of Christ;

Romans 6:1
What shall we say then? Are we to continue in sin so that grace may increase? 2May it never be! How shall we who died to sin still live in it?...

Reflection

SERAPHINITE

Seraphinite gemstone is a dark-green stone that plays beautifully with light. Seraphinite, the gem variety of clinochlore and found in Eastern Siberia. Seraphinite hardness on the Mohs scale is 2-2.5. Seraphinite from Russia displays feathery green silver iridescence leafy patterns so unique to this gemstone. Seraphinite is gem family of Clinochlore which has similar fibers as charoite another famous Russian gemstone.

Day Eight
THE TRUE INTEGRITY OF THE HEART

The true integrity of the heart is revealed through our mouths. You see, scripture says "Out of the abundance (overflow) of the heart the mouth speaks". Unfortunately, that means that negativity flows out of some hearts and manifests itself as evil, lies, backbiting, jealousy, envy, manipulation and chaos. This negativity should not flow from the mouths of believers. Bitter and sweet water does not flow out of the same fountain. So yes, the true integrity and character of our hearts is revealed through our speech - from our mouths as our 2 lips part. Out of it flows life or out of it flows death. The Word declares that it's not what goes in a man that defiles him but what comes out of the man.

So, let's be clear, what you allow to come out of you is an indicator of what you have allowed to go into you. We must protect our eyes, our ears and our hearts from receiving things that are against God's Word and allowing it to take root in our hearts. It's your choice - just know that one of two things will occur: either a heart that heals will be revealed or a heart that needs to be healed will be revealed. Don't allow your speech to betray you.

Afterthought

1. We are all different. God may convict one person of something that He may not have convicted you of, but even with that said, I want you to discuss what things you have allowed to enter into your mind through your 5 senses. Have these things sharpened your walk with God or have they made you insensitive to the presence of God?

2. What things have you said today or this week that you may need to repent and take back?

3. How does the words you say allow you to be a better spokesperson for the Kingdom?

Proverbs 18:21
Death and life are in the power of the tongue: and they that love it shall eat the fruit thereof.

Reflection

MOTHER OF PEARL

Mother of Pearl also known as "MOP," is the thin inner nacreous layer of a mollusk shell. It can have a base color of white, cream, or gray with a beautiful iridescent play-of-color. Mother of pearl has been used to produce jewelry and buttons. It has been used for fancy inlay work on musical instruments and furniture. It was much more widely used before plastic manufacturing became common.

WELL DONE

Our ultimate goal should be to live in such a way that in the end we hear 2 very small yet powerful words ... WELL DONE.

We can not become so entangled in this present, temporary world just so we can hear you are beautiful, you're sexy, wow you got it going on, etc. THIS WORLD IS TEMPORARY, but God is eternal. Our possessions (houses, land, money, degrees, careers, cars) are temporary, our relationships (marriage, friendships) are temporary, even our desires are temporary. It would be a shame to pour out, to complete empty yourself to these things, to gain the whole world and lose our souls. God is requiring us to completely pursue him with the goal of pleasing him and hearing him saying well done. What are you doing today to hear, "Well Done"?

Afterthought

1. Name some things that need to go in the category, "TEMPORARY" that you currently may have in the "PERMANENT ZONE".

2. What do the words Well Done mean to you? How does this currently reflect in your life?

2 Corinthians 4:18 (NIV)

So we fix our eyes not on what is seen, but on what is unseen, since what is seen is temporary, but what is unseen is eternal.

Reflection

PEANUT WOOD

Peanut Wood is a variety of petrified wood, where the shape and structure of the wood is pre- served when the original organic material is replaced by quartz.

Day Ten

LIVE AND LEARN

The term "to live and learn" means just that. What you have previously learned should be an experience you no longer want to live. You would think the Israelites would have finally learned their lesson, but time and time again God rescued them. I'm sure God feels the same way today about us. Time and time again we go about our lives, making decisions and mistakes and oftentimes the pattern of behavior that leads to those same mistakes goes unchanged. But today, you must determine in your heart, that not only will I live, but I will learn as well. I will learn from my mistakes (and even the mistakes of my forefathers) and say enough is enough! It's your choice, you really don't have to keep making the same decisions and choosing the same type of people or things to be in your life.

My prayer for you is that you will be of good courage as you walk in Faith. Even when those giants (divorce, poverty, sickness, depression, anxiety, fear, low self-esteem, and the other cousins of these issues) are staring you straight in the face, be reminded of what God has said, slay that giant with The Word of God and keep walking in Faith. Faith= Obedience. Don't cower in the face of the Giant. Be the overcomer God empowered you to be!

Afterthought

1. What patterns have you noticed in your life that require you to think differently and ultimately do differently?

2. What are some giants you feel you currently have in your life that need to be slayed by your Faith so you can walk in courage?

1 Corinthians 13:11
When I was a child, I spoke like a child, I thought like a child, I reasoned like a child. When I became a man, I gave up childish ways.

Reflection

ORTHOCLASE

Orthoclase is a transparent yellow feldspar resembling citrine quartz or yellow beryl, found primarily in Madagascar.

— Day Eleven —
GIANTSLAYERS

It's impossible for us to love like God wants us to without praying for a new heart. Loving as God has commanded means you can't decide to change your mind and stop loving if you do not get the response you want from the other person. We are to love while expecting nothing in return. Our old, wounded hearts do not have the capacity to love like this.

When you really understand who you are in God and that you are more than a conqueror because you are one with Him, then your religion will move to reality, your hype to hope and your fear to Faith. You really are the righteousness of God. Now that you know, your life must line up with this Truth.
God has not forgotten you and He has not forsaken you. Hold onto the promises he has made to you. Do not allow your present circumstance to dictate to your emotions or the Words that come out of your mouth as it will be contradictory to the hope you have maintained to this very point. DON'T GIVE UP NOW!!

When I turned to my morning reading this confirmed I needed to share that.......

Hebrews 6:10 AMP
For God is not unrighteous to forget or overlook your labor and the love which you have shown for His name's sake in ministering to the needs of the saints (His own consecrated people), as you still do.

Afterthought

1. Be honest what unmet expectations are you experiencing right now? Are there any expectations you believe God has of you that you are not living up to?

2. What words do you need to cast down as a result of emotionally declaring them?

3. What truth do you now need to stand on? Write it down

Psalms 51:10*(NLT)*
Create in me a clean heart, O God.
Renew a loyal spirit within me.

Reflection

DIAMOND

Diamond, the hardest known natural material, is a transparent carbon crystal. Diamond is famed not only for its superb hardness, but also for its high refractive index and dispersion.

— Day Twelve —
GUARANTEED VICTORY

1 Chronicles 14:10 AMP
David asked God, Shall I go up against the Philistines? And will You deliver them into my hand? And the Lord said, Go up, and I will deliver them into your hand.

Many times, instead of being like David, we make a decision on our own - then ask God to bless our decision. We move forward on a hope, on a whim - and then become disappointed if God never responds. But, there is a way to have victory every time, be like David, inquire of God first, wait for an answer and when he replies, whatever the reply is (even if you don't like it), if you follow it, you will have GUARANTEED VICTORY!!

#GUARANTEEDVICTORY

Afterthought

1. Can you recall a time that you made a decision without God that resulted in an epic failure? Yes, EPIC FAILURE - because it hurt so bad, it cost so much and you were totally vested in it. (Oh, I have a few of them.) Today, search, write, learn and walk in Victory!

Proverbs 3:6(NLT)
Seek his will in all you do,
and he will show you which path to take

Reflection

SPHALERITE

Sphalerite is a rare collector's gem which has exceptional dispersion (also known as fire). In fact its dispersion rating is three times as high as that for diamond.

Day Thirteen

GO GET THE WEALTH

Deuteronomy 8:18 AMP
But you shall [earnestly] remember the Lord your God, for it is He Who gives you power to get wealth, that He may establish His covenant which He swore to your fathers, as it is this day.

Our prayer should be.......Lord reveal to us how to use the power you've given us to obtain wealth. Every skill, talent, ability and gift that has been lying dormant I awaken it now that it may be used to bring Glory to God and wealth to me so that I can leave an inheritance for my children's children, be a blessing to others and be a Funder of the Kingdom!

Be sincere in your declaration. We have believed a poor man's gospel far too long as well as believing that your prosperity is going to fall out of the sky. No, God wants to work through you. He has given us so much and now it's time to use it. Your motivation needs to be if God gave it to me then I need to use it to bring him glory.

Afterthought

1. If it is God who gives us the ability to get wealth, who should be the receiver of the first fruits of this wealth?

2. What skills or talents have you allowed to lay dormant? What has caused you to put these things on the back burner? What will it take for you to move beyond this point without regrets?

Matthew 25:14-30 (NKJV)
"For the kingdom of heaven is like a man traveling to a far country, who called his own servants and delivered his goods to them. 15 And to one he gave five talents, to another two, and to another one, to each according to his own ability; and immediately he went on a journey. 16 Then he who had received the five talents went and traded with them, and made another five talents. 17 And likewise he who had received two gained two more also. 18 But he who had received one went and dug in the ground, and hid his lord's money. 19 After a long time the lord of those servants came and settled accounts with them.

20 "So he who had received five talents came and brought five other talents, saying, 'Lord, you delivered to me five talents; look, I have gained five more talents besides them.'

21 His lord said to him, 'Well done, good and faithful servant; you were faithful over a few things, I will make you ruler over many things. Enter into the joy of your lord.' 22 He also who had received two talents came and said, 'Lord, you delivered to me two talents; look, I have gained two more talents besides them.' 23 His lord said to him, 'Well done, good and faithful servant; you have been faithful over a few things, I will make you ruler over many things. Enter into the joy of your lord.'

24 "Then he who had received the one talent came and said, 'Lord, I knew you to be a hard man, reaping where you have not sown, and gathering where you have not scattered seed. 25 And I was afraid, and went and hid your talent in the ground. Look, there you have what is yours.'

26 "But his lord answered and said to him, 'You wicked and lazy servant, you knew that I reap where I have not sown, and gather where I have not scattered seed. 27 So you ought to have deposited my money with the bankers, and at my coming I would have received back my own with interest. 28 Therefore take the talent from him, and give it to him who has ten talents.

29 'For to everyone who has, more will be given, and he will have abundance; but from him who does not have, even what he has will be taken away. 30 And cast the unprofitable servant into the outer darkness. There will be weeping and gnashing of teeth.'.

Reflection

FLOURITE

Fluorite is a mineral with a veritable plethora of brilliant colors that include purple, blue, green, yellow, colorless, brown, pink and orange.

Day Fourteen

FEAR GO!

Jewels, we can live a life without fear. Try to get to the root of your fear and anxiety. Most likely it's something that's out of your control. EX. Time, weather, disease etc. One writer wrote that: Fear is FALSE EVIDENCE APPEARING REAL,

I say that Fear is CONTAMINATED FAITH! The point is Fear uses circumstances or what you perceive as your reality, Faith causes you to believe someone higher than you. The promise is, if he said it, it will come to pass because He can't lie and He doesn't fail. Who's report do you believe? And who/what do you trust?

If we are honest, at times what we are experiencing has nothing to do with a fear problem but a control problem. If we can't control that circumstance we become fearful. Hear a word from experience: The only person we can control is ourselves. God gave each person a choice and unfortunately there are times people choose things with which we disagree. Don't allow someone else's choice send you into a fear whirlwind. Next, believe that everything else is on God - either we trust Him or we don't. Choose to live in freedom not fear.

2 Corinthians 5:7 KJV
For we walk by Faith and not by sight
Hebrews 12:2
Looking unto Jesus the author and finisher of our faith;

Afterthought

1. How has fear paralyzed you?

2. What steps will you begin to take to walk in Faith vs Fear?

2 Timothy 1:7
*For God hath not given us the spirit of fear;
but of power, and of love, and of a sound mind*

Reflection

CARNELIAN

Carnelian is a glassy, translucent gemstone that is typically light brownish-red to deep transparent stone. Carnelian belongs to the quartz family of gems and has been called Red agate or Red chalcedony in modern times. Most cabochon Carnelian are opaque with a domed top and flat bottom.

Day Fifteen

JEHOVAH-GOD

Jewels, once and for all I'm going to crush thus lie that the enemy has the body of Christ believing. GOD DOES NOT MAKE YOU SICK, GOD DOES NOT SEND EVIL TO YOU TO TEACH YOU A LESSON and GOD NEVER GIVES YOU SOMETHING THAT'S A TRICK QUESTION. If either of these were true, then how could you ever trust this God and even go to him to receive the opposite. If you are sick, would you go to the same person for healing who made you sick? Would you go to him for prosperity if he sent poverty your way? Would you go to him for freedom if he put you in bondage to teach you a lesson? I wouldn't - and you don't have to either, because that's NOT the kind of God we serve.

He really is the God that healeth thee - Jehovah Rohi.
He is the shepherd who supplies your needs - Jehovah Jireh.
He is the I AM - He can do anything but fail.
He is good.
Now choose to be free!

Afterthought

1. As you read this, have you considered perhaps the wrong teaching you have received that you need to denounce in order that you can receive the fullness of God?

2. Can you think of others teachings you may have received that were in order or against the nature of God?

3. Will you commit to study to show yourself approved?

Pray: Father forgive me for receiving teaching that was not in alignment with your Word. I denounce anything that I have received as truth that you make me sick or that you punish me. You are my healer and I receive your healing. I come into the truth that my decisions lead to consequences whether good or bad and that I reap what I sow. Today I pray to reap all the good seeds I have sown and ask for your grace as I endure consequences of bad decisions that I knew were against your will. Thank God that I can be transformed by the renewing of my mind.

Exodus 15:26
.....*I am the Lord that healeth thee*

Reflection

JADE

Natural Jade gems were discovered over 7000 years ago. Jade was very popular in ancient times for its toughness and was used for making tools and weapons.

− Day Sixteen −
GOD CAN BE TRUSTED

If God said it, it must come to pass. Psalms 138:8 says, God will perfect that which concerns you. That assignment, that dream, that vision - He's going to cause it to mature, to grow up and to be fruitful. He's perfecting it and He's perfecting you for it. Don't be weary... you're just in the perfecting process. To perfect does not mean without flaw or without mistakes but rather to mature and/or to complete. Don't you get it? If God said it, He will cause it to be complete in your life. We can rest assured on the promises and the Word of God. He is faithful, he's not like man, He keeps every Word, He keeps every promise and He can't lie neither can He fail. Your very existence is about God perfecting something in your life.

I declare that you will establish yourself as a witness in the Earth. A witness of God revealing His purpose for your life and completing what He has begun in you.

Afterthought

1. What part of your perfecting process has you believing that you won't complete the assignment for your life?

REPEAT AFTER ME: I am who God says I am, I will do all that He has destined for me to do, I am fully capable and qualified to fulfill the assignment for my life. He chose me.

Numbers 23:19
God is not a man, that he should lie; neither the son of man, that he should repent: hath he said, and shall he not do it? or hath he spoken, and shall he not make it good?

Reflection

SAPPHIRE

There are many reasons why the sapphire, also known as the stone of wisdom and royalty, is a popular choice. The late Princess Diana's engagement ring was a 18 caret oval Sapphire stone. The gem of gems is a jewel steeped in the history of nearly every religion. It is the birthstone for those born in September, and it is only second in hardness to the diamond. Sapphires are a top choice for jewelers, collectors, or those who simply want to adorn themselves with the beloved stone.

-Day Seventeen-
I AM NOT A VICTIM

Jewels, we must destroy, demolish, dismantle and pull down the stronghold of "VICTIM". No, it should not have happened, but you made it, you're still here, and you are still alive. Now, there are also times when we play the victim but know we are the ones who made the decision knowing full well we knew it was a bad choice when we made it. Put on your big girl panties and dust yourself off. You win and you are a victor! But guess what, no one can pray this off of you or cast it out of you - YOU must make a decision to pull it down. You already have the ability and the strength you need to do it through the Holy Ghost. Now go on and PULLLLLLLLLLLL!!!!!!!!!

Yes pull baby, pull that depression down, pull that self-pity down, pull that low self-esteem down, pull that low confidence down, pull down that poverty mindset, pull down every word curse spoken against your destiny, pull down your past, pull down those old memories that keep you in those old negative cycles, PULL IT DOWN!!!! The Bible says in Mark 11:23 NIV - Truly I tell you, if anyone says to this mountain, Go, throw yourself into the sea, and does not doubt in their heart but believes that what they say will happen, it will be done for them.

Afterthought

1. Do you believe what you say? Have you told yourself lies that you will no longer believe that power in your tongue?

2. What mountains do you need to speak to? What strongholds do you need to pull down in order to be your best self? Go ahead, write them down and be honest.

Proverbs 18:21 KJV
Death and life are in the power of the tongue,
and those who love it will eat its fruit.

Reflection

SILVER

Silver is the metallic element with the atomic number 47. A soft, white, lustrous transition metal, it exhibits the highest electrical conductivity, thermal conductivity, and reflectivity of any metal. The metal is found in the Earth's crust in the pure, free elemental form ("native silver"), as an alloy with gold and other metals, and in minerals such as argentite and chlorargyrite. Most silver is produced as a byproduct of copper, gold, lead, and zinc refining. As one of the seven metals of antiquity, silver has had an enduring role in most human

-Day Eighteen-
DON'T FALL FOR THE TRAP!

It's proof of who you are, of who God says you are, when the enemy sets traps for you. The enemy wouldn't waste his time with you if you were not a threat. But just know, NO WEAPON FORMED AGAINST YOU WILL PROSPER! It's only a distraction to take your mind and eyes off of God. Don't fall for the trap!

Be the you God created you to be, the unashamed, unapologetic, full of Joy, Fearfully and Wonderfully Made you. The Called and Chosen by God You. The unstoppable you. People will not like you for being you. They will hate that others like you. They won't know *why* they don't like you, but just keep being you. When you present to the world the real you, you exhibit the image of God. Yes you, the royal and peculiar apple of God's eye.

"You make others respect God's creation (you) when you refuse to succumb to their (whoever they are) box!"

Afterthought

1. Take some time to write out who you are, the you even no one is watching.

2. Now that you have completed that, what adjustments if any do you need to make to be your best self? Remember you are to exhibit in the Earth the image of God, are you doing this consistently? If not why not? If so, your diligence will work in your favor.

1 Peter 2:9 KJV
But ye are a chosen generation, a royal priesthood, an holy nation, a peculiar people, that ye should shew forth the praises of him who hath called you out of darkness into his marvelous light.

Reflection

SUNSTONE

Sunstone is a member of the Feldspar family, and is named for its warm shades of gold, orange, reds and browns that sparkle like the sun. Inclusions of Goethite or Hematite refract light between the different crystal layers and produce an iridescent effect as the stone is viewed from various angles. Sunstone may be clear and transparent, or opaque, and is readily available on the market. Clean red specimens, however, are rare.

Day Nineteen

HIS REFLECTION

I'm not sure how many of you all remember the commercial for the doll called MY BUDDY. The theme song/jingle for it was, "My buddy, my buddy, wherever I go he goes, my buddy". Well, let's be reminded as we walk out our journeys with the Lord, that wherever we go HE goes. You can not compartmentalize Him and take Him only to places you want Him to go. He's omnipresent everywhere at the same time. He's omnipotent all powerful and he's omniscient all knowing.

If we are to ever win a dying world to the saving power of the Lord Jesus Christ then what we say must be in agreement with the Word but also mirror what we do. It's easy to be a hearer of the Word but to walk by Faith takes action and requires us to be a doer of the Word. I challenge you to be quick to hear and slow to speak that your words don't outrun your ability.

Afterthought

1. Have you ever been to a place that something on the inside of you suggested that you should not be there?

2. What did that feel like?

3. How will you use this information in the future?

1 Corinthians 6:17
But the person who is united to the Lord becomes one spirit with Him.

Reflection

AFGHANITE

Afghanite is an extremely rare collector gem that is usually found as a blue crystal. It is an extremely complex mineral and can be found in many forms. As the name suggests this mineral is mainly found in Afghanistan. When this gem is placed under UV light, it goes from a blue gem into an electric orange florescent stone.

-Day Twenty-
BE HEALED AND MOVE ON!

Do you know to be healed is a choice? God wants to heal you and that broken heart and wounded spirit. But if you want to keep walking around being mean and bitter, with a chip on your shoulder it's your choice. But your healing begins with honesty, some of the things we experienced came to be because we allowed them to. Yes, God will deal with them, but it's not your job. Take the accountability for allowing them in, in the first place. Heal and move on!

I am reminded of the woman with the issue of blood in Mark 5, the Bible says after she heard about Jesus she began to seek after him for her healing. She had to choose to believe that He was a healer. After that choice she had to move towards him. Faith without works is dead. Just as she had to make a choice so do you. She could have remained a victim of 12 years with her infirmity or she could choose to believe what others were talking about in regards to this man named Jesus.

Guess what? He is no respecter of persons, what He did for the woman with the issue of blood He will do for you, if only you believe. Just know your healing could be immediate or it could be a process, either way you must believe you are healed regardless how you feel. The pain of the breakup, divorce or death may still be there but I promise you, one day, you will look back at this time and say to yourself that it had to be God that brought you through it. For now, allow the pain to remind you that you are alive and that better days are ahead.

Afterthought

1. Is there an area in your life that you need to choose to be healed? What is it?

2. What do you need to do to pursue your healing?

3. How will your healing impact your life?

Jeremiah 17:14
Heal me, O Lord, and I shall be healed;
save me, and I shall be saved:
for thou art my praise.

Reflection

TURQUOISE

Turquoise is an opaque, blue-to-green mineral that is a hydrated phosphate of copper and aluminum. It is rare and valuable in finer grades and has been prized as a gemstone and ornamental stone for thousands of years owing to its unique hue.

Day Twenty One
WHEN GOD DOES IT

When God does it, hear me clearly, WHEN GOD DOES IT, NOBODYYYYYYY and I mean nobody can get the credit BUT GOD! He does all things well. The favor of God is better than anything in the world. GOD IS A RESTORER!!!!!! So instead of asking God for stuff, houses, cars, lands, shoes, husbands, children etc pray to activate the favor of God that's on your life. With favor someone may want to give you a house or a car with no payments. Perhaps favor will place you in position to be found by your husband. Never discredit the power of favor. Favor will have people paying for things for you because they heard God, so they decided to respond in Faith.

Now, favor isn't a replacement of faith neither is it a substitute for wisdom. In all things, we are to acknowledge God and He will direct our paths. I think about all the times people counted me out, teen mom, lived in the projects, divorced, remarried etc but favor will close the mouths of the naysayers. When you walk in obedience to God, He will restore you the years you thought you lost with wrong decisions, mistakes and ill-willed people. God will stop at nothing in order for his glory to be revealed in your life.

Afterthought

1. What are things you believed you lost?

2. Have you seen those things restored?

3. How will you pray differently now?

Joel 2:25

And I will restore to you the years that the locust hath eaten, the cankerworm, and the caterpillar, and the palmerworm, my great army which I sent among you.

Reflection

ZIRCON

Zircon is a natural gemstone that is often confused with the man-made Cubic Zirconia. Please be aware that these are two completely different minerals. Zircon is a beautiful natural gemstone that has the fire of a Diamond and comes in many colors.

-Day Twenty Two-
WHAT'S YOUR VALUE?

Everything/everyone has a value. Value is determined by the previous owner of something and how much someone is willing to pay for it. Now think about that, if you say Jesus is your owner and then base that on how much he paid for you, how valuable does that make you? PRICELESS! That information alone should prevent us from allowing others to define us. They are not the creator and many times those who don't have your best future in mind will speak words to get you off track of your destiny. We can no Longer give access into our lives of those individuals who are destiny robbers and dream killers. Today, decide that you will not allow others to define or determine your value. Just think you were so priceless that you were worth dying for.

DECLARATION: I am priceless to God therefore I will carry myself as such. I am a daughter of the King.

Afterthought

1. Give some thought to this question....Who am I? How do I introduce myself? Ask a few very close about how they perceive you? What does my resume say about me? What does my attitude say about me? What do I wear say about me?

2. Lastly, how does God describe you? What has he said about you? Has he spoken anything directly? If so write it down.

Jeremiah 1:5
"Before I formed you in the womb I knew you, before you were born I set you apart"

Reflection

SHELLSTONES

Shellstones most often come from the lining of clam shells, usually in California, Mexico, or Japan. The shells vary in grade depending on whether they are taken from the edge of the shell (highest grade), middle, or near the joint (lowest).

Day Twenty Three
IF

I think about all the 'IF'S" in my life. At times the enemy will try to consume you with the thoughts of shoulda, woulda, coulda but I took those times and made them a testimony of God's grace. There's a song that has the lyrics by Tye Tribbett "The devil thought he had me, He thought my life was over, He thought by now I'd give up, He thought I had no more". After listening to that song on repeat over and over again I came to this resolve:

IF I was successful with the suicide I wouldn't be here

IF I had allowed the molestation to manipulate my mind I would be homosexual

IF I had allowed rejection to matter I would be in the world and done with God and His church.

IF I had allowed the depression to isolate me I would be in the psych ward still today

IF I had allowed my bad choices and decisions to shame me I would be lonely…….
BUT GOD!

All of that worked for my good, it worked for me and today I know that God was, is and will continue to be very intentional concerning me.

Afterthought

1. What are your "IF'S"?

2. Take some time to write our your personal testimony. Remember no matter what the enemy says no one can take away your testimony or your victory report. You survived, you overcame and you have the story to tell it. Own it, it's yours to write.

Exodus 14:13
Moses answered the people, "Do not be afraid. Stand firm and you will see the deliverance the Lord will bring you today. **The Egyptians you see today you will never see again.**

Reflection

MALACHITE

This mineral was given this name due to its resemblance to the leaves of the mallow plant.[6] Malachite was extensively mined at the Greate Orme mines in the Britain 3,800 years ago using stone and bone tools. Archeological evidence indicates that mining activity ended around 600 B.C.E with up to 1,760 tons of copper being produced from the mined Malachite.[7][8]Archeological evidence indicates that the mineral has been mined and smelted to obtain copper at Timna Valley in Israel for over 3,000 years.[9] Since then, malachite has been used as both an ornamental stone and as a gemstone.

Day Twenty Four
HEALING IS OURS

I really do believe that the Blood of Jesus still has power. I really do believe that by His stripes we were healed. I really do believe that healing is our portion. I really do believe that sickness if from the devil and not apart of God's intention for our lives. Jesus came to the Earth so that we can have life abundantly. If you are ever facing a health crisis you have to remain unshaken and your hope must remain in the truth that "God can still be trusted" taken from my friend Jackie Tripp. Glue those words to your heart, GOD CAN STILL BE TRUSTED.

There was a time in my life, that was one of the most trying times when it comes to believing God for healing. My mother had been sick in the hospital from what was initially pneumonia. This trial lasted for 4 years. Four years doesn't seem long to some but to me it was an eternity watching her suffer, uncomfortable and bed ridden. There were times I wouldn't allow others to visit her because I didn't want others around who didn't believe like me for her healing. Even Jesus did this in scriptures when he had to have others removed out of the room before he healed her. You may find yourself in a similar situation, either way surround yourself with like believers. Don't get discouraged or dismayed, stand on the Word of God.

Luke 8:40-42, 49-55:
[40] Now when Jesus returned, a crowd welcomed him, for they were all expecting him. [41] Then a man named Jairus, a ruler of the synagogue, came and fell at Jesus' feet, pleading with him to come to his house [42] because his only daughter, a girl of about twelve, was dying. As Jesus was on his way, the crowds almost crushed him....
[49] While Jesus was still speaking, someone came from the house of Jairus, the synagogue ruler. "Your daughter is dead," he said. "Don't bother the teacher any more."
[50] Hearing this, Jesus said to Jairus, "Don't be afraid; just believe, and she will be healed."
[51] When he arrived at the house of Jairus, he did not let anyone go in with him except Peter, John and James, and the child's father and mother. [52] Meanwhile, all the people were wailing and mourning for her. "Stop wailing," Jesus said. "She is not dead but asleep."
[53] They laughed at him, knowing that she was dead. [54] But he took her by the hand and said, "My child, get up!" [55] Her spirit returned, and at once she stood up. Then Jesus told them to give her something to eat

Decree: I declare that my emotions will line up with my faith. That we are healed. Every generational curse if broken and I sever the bloodline with the word of the spirit. I now have new blood and a new DNA through Christ Jesus. I speak a blessing of Health over my family and a thousand generations forward in Jesus Name. God you get the glory out of this.

Afterthought

1. Gather a list of scriptures from the Bible concerning healing and declare those scriptures over your life, your children and your loved ones. Use the authority God has given you. Your weapon is the Word of God.

2 Corinthians 10:4
For the weapons of our warfare are not carnal, but mighty through God to the pulling down of strong holds.

Reflection

GARNET

Garnet is one of the most versatile gemstones available and are found in multiple countries. Garnet is actually the name given to an entire family of gemstones. You may already know of the red garnet stone, but did you know there are different garnet colors? You will find green garnet, blue garnet, purple, yellow and even orange garnet.

Day Twenty Five
YOU JUST DO YOU

There's a new phrase that is going around that says: "You just do you" or I'm just going to do me. Well I don't believe that those who have been bought with a price can just "do them". We have to be careful that by following the trends of society that we reject the plans of God and fail to do what God has called us to do. That we do so much of "us", that it's no longer about God but all about us. I want a new house, I want a new job, I want a new relationship, I want to be married, I want a divorce, I want to do what I want to do when I want to do it. Having desires isn't the issue, but when those desires consume us so much that we become deaf to the voice of God and you are being led by the voices of society then we have missed the mark.

The Bible clearly tells us in Proverbs 3:6 - In all thy ways **acknowledge Him**, And **He will direct** thy **paths** (emphasis added). This was also Jonah's issue, but because of God's love and his intent on him carrying out his mission, Jonah was found in a belly of fish, a deep dark place that after that was done he still had no choice but to DO GOD!. This all could have been avoided by a simple yes, and an internal agreement of "Not my will but your will be done".

Doing you means you remain prideful, unforgiving, slothful, stagnant, unfruitful, unaccountable, unfaithful, unteachable and ultimately unGodly. In contrast when we allow God to lead and we follow, He is glorified and we are edified.

Afterthought

1. What does "just do you" mean to you?

2. Have you ever found yourself in a situation where you decided to just "do you"? How did this impact your life? (Positively or negatively)

3. Is there anything you can definitely say you learned from this experience?

Ephesians 4:13
Till we all come in the unity of the faith, and of the knowledge of the Son of God, to a perfect man, to the measure of the stature of the fullness of Christ:

Reflection

CALLIGRAPHY

Calligraphy Stone is an amazing looking gem with patterns that look like writing. It is also known as the holy stone, Script Stone and Elephant Skin Jasper. it is fossil material of some type, and the two different colors are of different hardnesses. There is no agreement as to whether it is fossilized grasses & reeds, fossilized shell, or some combination of both. Some sources say it is a jasper and other sources say it is not really a jasper but a mixture of shells, sand, and limonite.

Day Twenty Six
YOU ARE A DESIGNER'S ORIGINAL

You must become comfortable with how God created you. Stop trying to be like others and fit in. You are fearfully and wonderfully made. As you walk in your God created self, you won't have to apologize any more, people will just have to expand their capacity to have you in their lives. Have you ever tried to be someone else just to fit in? Over time, this becomes overwhelming and time consuming.

The anxiety of trying to remember who you pretend to be versus your real self. Look, it's time out for that. Those days are over. Put that behind you. In fact, did you know the anointing on your life is connected to your God created, original self? That's right, your anointing is connect to you, not the made up, false image you. The real people God has connected to you will show up because they are drawn to the real you. I love my loud, funny, quirky self and people know without wavering that that's exactly who they are going to get. I love being me. I can't imagine the world without me. Break the box, you are a designers original. I make no apologies.

Afterthought

1. Can you remember the first time you dealt with rejection? What was it connected to? What was your plan of action after this?

2. Do you still deal with rejection? How can you deal with this differently now?

3. What is your perception of yourself?

4. What was your relationship like with your parents? Did they affirm who you are? What are things you heard? Do you agree or disagree?

5. What is Gods perception of you?

Jeremiah 1:5 (NIV)
Before I formed you in the womb I knew you, before you were born I set you apart; I appointed you as a prophet to the nation

Reflection

CAVANSITE

Cavansite is greenish-blue to sea-blue stone that is extremely vibrant. It is generally found in the market as a specimen as it is almost impossible to cut a gemstone from this mineral. Only discovered in the past few decades, cavansite is found primarily in Poona, India and Oregon in the US. Its hardness is 3-4 so it is very soft. Although it was only discovered a few decades ago, Cavansite is a highly popular and widely sought-after mineral.

Day Twenty Seven
THE FINISH LINE

Many ask the question "how do you get to the finish line in your walk with God?". Well my response to that is by following His Word and by an instruction of God. The Bible says the Word is a lamp into our feet and a light unto our path.

What that means is, we can be carrying out a task but unless God illuminates that path and brings light unto that path we are literally walking blindly and walking in vain. You see the Bible also says, "If you acknowledge me in all of your ways I will direct your path".

Many of us are trying to reach the finish line and cross the finish line without a Word from God or without direction. We find in scripture many times Jesus saying "I come to do the work of my father....".

Jesus had a plan and a mission to accomplish. Regardless of what things looked like or how it seemed he Had to accomplish that which he was sent to do. In fact at one time he was asking, Father is there any way this cup can pass from me? BUT not my will but your will be done. Do you understand that we have the same mandate? You and I were created for a specific reason and purpose. It's time to find out what that is in order to hear "Well done my good and Faithful servant".

We must make a habit of submission to God in order to cross our destined finished line. Paul could confidently say, "I've kept the Faith, I've finished my course". Essentially Paul was saying I kept a habit of Obedience.

At the end of the day it's not our praise, our shout, our dance, keyboards, guitars or maracas that's gonna get us to the finish line. BUT it is our obedience. Faith is the only thing that pleases God. Faith = Obedience.

1. Are there things happening in your life that are interfering with your obedience?

2. What radical changes do you need to quickly make?

3. What changes could be more harder than others?

4. What do you think it would cost you to walk in complete obedience to the best of your ability?

Luke 22:42
Father, if thou be willing, remove this cup from me: nevertheless not my will, but thine, be done

Reflection

APATITE

Apatite is one of the defining minerals on the MOHS scale of hardness (5) so it is important in gemology. It is a very common mineral and gem quality crystals can be found in Brazil, Indian ,Kenya, Mexico, Madagascar, Burma, Norway, South Africa and the USA. Some of the most sought after Apatite has a strong neon blue green color that rivals the Paraiba Tourmaline. If it is cut into a domed Cabochon gem, in some cases it can exhibit a cat's eye effect known as Chatoyancy.

Day Twenty Eight

IT DOESN'T FEEL GOOD, BUT IT'S FOR MY GOOD

Have you ever felt like you knew the plan for your life but what you were experiencing looks nothing like that plan? I've been there. Through some of our most difficult life seasons we must learn to trust God.

When we are walking through the valley of the shadow of death we must trust God. We must trust that he knows best. Do we trust that he won't put more on us than we can handle? Do we know that he's our front and our rear guard? Do we know he already has the answers and if he owns a cattle on a thousand hills he can meet your need with just one. We have to know that all things, not some things, not some of the time but all things even those things that you thought you already had worked out, you already had a plan for it but then it flopped, because god says I know the thoughts and plans I think towards you and that was not in the plan for this appointed time.

Oh yes, there is a time but we have to trust god's timing. There are things now that if you look back over your life on how difficult a certain season was in your life, seems like you would never come through. But, you now see how god orchestrated that thing for your now season. The bankruptcy had to happen, the divorce had to happen, the sickness had to happen, the hurt had to happen so that you would know who is your keeper, where your help comes from, so that you would learn humility because you were walking in pride. You can think of so many other reasons why if you're honest. A pharmacist at times are mixing together 2 deadly chemicals to produce something beneficial that individually and of themselves are poison. That's just how it is, some of our mess from our past in and of itself is poison but when it's laced with the mercy and grace of god it produces a testimony. All of that worked together that you will walk in your purpose, with a story of victory!

Afterthought

1. What's your story/stories of victory? Have you ever written it down? Now would be a great time.

Genesis 50:20
You intended to harm me, but God intended it for good to accomplish what is now being done, the saving of many lives.

Reflection

AMMOLITE

Ammolite is a unique and wonderful semi-precious gemstone that is actually formed from a fossilized sea creature. It is believed that these fossils formed over 65 million years ago and are commonly found in Canada.

Day Twenty Nine
IT'S NO SECRET, I'M PREGNANT!

This is not as deep as we think, but if you are pregnant with something whether that is a human child, a business venture or vision, it is a process. Merriam-Webster defines process as: a natural phenomenon marked by gradual changes that lead toward a particular result. You are excited about what's to come but the pregnancy is a process. It doesn't always feel good, you are uncomfortable, morning sickness, lack of sleep, swollen legs and feet, wide nose, cramps, labor pain, stretch marks etc. IT'S NOT EASY. There is a process.

You are eating for two, you are responsible for someone other than yourself, and even after the baby is here you have to be responsible for what God has entrusted to you. You have to parent it. This child represents the DNA of the father and it represents the DNA of you, however you must be intentional about its growth. You say we want to be pregnant but do you really? I hear many while they are praying trying to remind God about what He said but what about your responsibility in the matter? Are you willing to give up your body for the sake of another? Are you willing to give up your wants and desires to produce a healthy child, business or vision? What are you willing to give up?

Our daily confession should be Luke 22:42 NOT MY WILL, BUT YOUR WILL BE DONE. We must whole-heartedly submit to PRESENT YOUR BODIES AS A LIVING SACRIFICE HOLY AND ACCEPTABLE UNTO GOD WHICH IS YOUR REASONABLE SERVICE Romans 12:1.

You see, you can not just give up in the middle of the pregnancy and say I don't want to be pregnant anymore that's called an ABORTION.

You can't just stop taking care of yourself, because someone else is dependent on you, that leads to miscarriage.

God needs people who are willing, and able to go full-term! God's Word promises us that We will reap if we faint not. Galatians 6:9.

1. Name something you believe God has given you to do?

2. Have you began? Started? Completed? Quit?

3. When the process is uncomfortable are you known to quit? If so what can you do different? If you haven't quit, what are you doing to empower others to go through the process?

Psalms 118:23 *(ESV)*
This is the LORD's doing, and it is wonderful to see.

Reflection

NATURAL AMBER

Natural Amber is mesmerizing. It is one of the earliest organic materials man used to adorn himself. We have been compelled to incorporate it into our art forms and adornments since the Stone Age. It was one of the first amulet stones in Asia. Amber is not strictly speaking a stone but resin. It is produced from tree resin from ancient pine forests. This resin was washed down rivers to the Baltic sea. The resin was fossilized over millions of years and became Amber.

Day Thirty
DON'T GET TIRED!

Gal 6:9 Don't become weary (tired, worn out, exhausted, fatigued, sapped, burnt-out, dog-tired, spent, drained) in doing well for you shall reap (receive, obtain, get, acquire, secure, realize) if you faint not.

I believe we are becoming weary because we have become religious. We are doing the same things over and over again. We are doing things of old but are not seeking God in the now. God is wanting to lead and guide us in the now. Isaiah 43:19 Behold, I am doing a new thing; now it springs forth, do you not perceive it? I will make a way in the wilderness and rivers in the desert. It's time to come out of the desert. God did say he will be your provision while you are in the desert but it's not your final destination. Many of us have become content and stuck between our start and our destination. But today you are reading this jewel nugget to empower you to oil that engine up, put yourself into gear and with all you got, full speed charge ahead towards what you heard or saw God speak to you and don't quit until you hear....ENTER IN.

Afterthought

1. Without limitations (time or money) what are the things you would be doing passionately?

2. Are there new connections you need to make in order to accomplish this?

3. Do you resist new relationships? Who do you need to forgive or let go of so you can walk in obedience to the call that's on your life?

4. Do you agree that there are times that we are our own hindrance to experience the blessing of God?

5. How have these 30 days shaped your life? What can you commit to do in order to walk in your new found identity as a Jewel of God?

Isaiah 43:19 (a)
Behold, I am doing a new thing, now it shall spring forth....

Reflection

Meet The Author

Evangelist Janet Stephens (affectionately known as Lady J) was born December 22, 1977 to Elder Jerry and Evangelist Jeanette Sanders, founding pastors of True Vine Church of Apostolic Church in Urbancrest, Ohio. Both parents are now sleeping and awaiting the resurrection of the saints. Lady J is honored to be a servant under the dynamic, anointed five-fold ministry of Apostle Terry Stephens II of Truth and Wholeness Ministries, who is also her husband. There she serves as an ordained Elder and is being nurtured and driven to walk in purpose and destiny. Lady J is a servant at heart and assists the ministry in any facet she can in equipping, and developing men, women and children alike to do the work of the ministry.

Lady J has a Bachelor's degree from The Ohio State University in social and behavior science and graduated from her studies in Biblical Counseling in April 2009 under the direction of Dr. Sandy and Apostle Greg Burkett of Marion Christian Center/Breakthrough Ministries. In 2013 she graduated from the Ministerial Alliance training through Rhema Christian Center under the direction of Apostle Lafayette Scales. Her secular job is with Franklin County Children Services as a supervisor, however her first ministry is to her husband and their blended family of six, Ja'Neyce, Ja'Nique, Tre, Jaylin, Andre and Maya. Janet has a heart for the unchurched and those who need to return to God. She has developed a love for teaching the word of God and is passionate about everyone learning about their purpose in life, establishing a vision for their life, and walking in destiny. Lady J has served in many areas of ministry administratively, teaching, preaching and in song. Her favorite scripture is Jeremiah 29:11 KJV For I know the thoughts that I think toward you, sayeth the LORD, thoughts of peace, and not of evil, to give you an expected end. Despite many challenges, it is the Lord's plans that prevail! You can tell in her step and in her smile that the Joy of the Lord is her strength, and that weeping had its night season but that her morning has come!

CONNECT WITH JANET STEPHENS (LADY J):
Email: ladyjstephens7@gmail.com

MANIFESTATION CHURCH:
1234 Demorest Rd
Columbus, Ohio 43204
614-321-5196

SOCIAL MEDIA
Facebook: Janet Stephens and Jewels by Lady J
Instagram: LadyJStephens
Twitter: Jewels by Lady J